A Practical Guide
for Praying Parents

A Practical Guide for Praying Parents

Erwin W. Lutzer

MOODY PUBLISHERS

CHICAGO

Edited by Amanda Cleary Eastep
Interior and cover design: Erik M. Peterson
Cover illustration of leaf frame copyright © 2019 by vectortwins / Shutterstock (1092403787).
All rights reserved.

Library of Congress Cataloging-in-Publication Data

Names: Lutzer, Erwin W., author.
Title: A practical guide for praying parents / Erwin W. Lutzer.
Description: Chicago : Moody Publishers, [2020] | Includes bibliographical
  references. | Summary: "Your best intentions can become effective
  intercessions for your children or grandchildren. Trade your lists of
  requests for Scripturally-based prayers that will immerse you in God's
  promises and will. A Practical Guide for Praying Parents will help you
  pray scriptural prayers that bring you closer to God and bless your
  children"-- Provided by publisher.
Identifiers: LCCN 2020004649 (print) | LCCN 2020004650 (ebook) | ISBN
  9780802420404 (paperback) | ISBN 9780802498977 (ebook)
Subjects: LCSH: Parents--Religious life. | Grandparents--Religious life. |
  Parents--Prayers and devotions. | Grandparents--Prayers and devotions. |
  Bible--Prayers.
Classification: LCC BV4529 .L88 2020 (print) | LCC BV4529 (ebook) | DDC
  248.3/2085--dc23
LC record available at https://lccn.loc.gov/2020004649
LC ebook record available at https://lccn.loc.gov/2020004650

Originally delivered by fleets of horse-drawn wagons, the affordable paperbacks from D. L. Moody's publishing house resourced the church and served everyday people. Now, after more than 125 years of publishing and ministry, Moody Publishers' mission remains the same—even if our delivery systems have changed a bit. For more information on other books (and resources) created from a biblical perspective, go to: www.moodypublishers.com or write to:

Moody Publishers
820 N. LaSalle Boulevard
Chicago, IL 60610

1 3 5 7 9 10 8 6 4 2

Printed in the United States of America

Bruce and Lori
Shay and Lynn
Ben and Lisa
We pass the torch to you

Contents

Foreword

Erwin Lutzer is one of the foremost Christian authors in the world. His books have instructed and inspired people around the globe. My friend has now taken aim at one of the most critical issues facing believers in Jesus today. In his new book, *A Practical Guide for Praying Parents*, he is helping us to understand the power of prayer as it pertains to the spiritual needs of our children.

Years ago my wife Carol and I went through a long dark tunnel that seemed to have no light at the end of it. Our oldest daughter rebelled against both us and God, leaving us bewildered and heartbroken. This was the model child that grew up in church with parents trying to serve the Lord. I made every effort to reason with her but all to no avail. It was then that my eyes were opened afresh to the fact that only God could change our daughter's heart. And He did!

Erwin Lutzer's new book will do more than just answer your questions with sound biblical truth. It will also draw you to the throne of grace where miracles happen as God responds to simple childlike faith. This book is a blessing from the Lord!

JIM CYMBALA
Author and Pastor, The Brooklyn Tabernacle

Introduction

Moreover, as for me, far be it from me that I should sin against the LORD by ceasing to pray for you" (1 Sam. 12:23). Those are the words of the Old Testament prophet Samuel who, in a single sentence, tells us two important truths: prayerlessness is a sin against the Lord, and we should pray without ceasing. If Samuel could speak to parents, I have no doubt that he would say:

It is a sin for you not to pray for your children!

Our children belong to God. If we want to honor them, the best way we can do that is to pray for them regularly, fervently, and optimistically, expecting God to answer. Do you love your children? Prove it by praying for them.

If I dare to be honest, often when we pray for our children, we either fall into meaningless repetition, or we submit a grocery list of requests to God. We hope that He'll respond to our wishes and desires. These types of prayers leave us unsatisfied, fretful, and uncertain as to whether or not we can trust God with the assignment we've just given Him.

Years ago, I would pray "need-based" prayers for our children. I was repeating myself and rehearsing the same lists of requests each day. Often, I confess, my prayers were boring, filled with uncertainty, and reduced to a meaningless exercise. Like many of you, I found myself in a rut as I prayed for my children and grandchildren.

Then it all changed.

I realized that if I pray Scripture, I can change the focus of my prayer each day; and what is more, I am echoing back to God that which is His will. Wouldn't such prayers stimulate our faith, bring glory to Him, and rid us of the repetition that Jesus warned us about? The answer is an unequivocal *yes*.

I now anticipate my time of prayer with enthusiasm, wondering exactly what I'll pray next. Best of all, my prayer time sinks deep roots into God's promises and His will. That kind of praying is effective, not just in moving God's heart toward us, but by giving us a deep-settled satisfaction that we've just connected with our heavenly Father.

This small book is intended . . .

- to help us as parents and grandparents pray scriptural prayers for our children.

- to help us be faithful even when it appears as if our prayers are not being answered.
- to combine prayer and worship in a way to meet our own need for God.

God has blessed my wife, Rebecca, and me with three married daughters, three sons-in-law, and eight lovely and lively grandchildren. Long ago I gave up on the idea of simply listing their names before God and asking Him to "bless" them. What I've chosen to do instead is pray for one grandchild one day a week beginning from the eldest to the youngest (praying for two on Saturday). Each week I choose a passage of Scripture to pray on their behalf. In other words, I often use the same passage for each child but adapt it to their needs and ages. When each grandchild is prayed for, I include their parents in that day's prayer.

I had the good fortune of having parents who prayed for all five of their children fervently and regularly. On their 70th wedding anniversary (they lived to celebrate their 77th anniversary before my father died at age 106), I asked my mother if she knew the names of all of her grandchildren and great-grandchildren. With a wave of her hand she said, "Oh yes, I have a prayer list and I pray for them; I mention their names to our heavenly Father every day!" When she died at age 102, there were dozens of names on her prayer list: her children, grandchildren, great-grandchildren, a few friends, and some missionaries! I believe that my ministry today is the result of my parents' prayers.

This book is intended to help you get started on what I hope will be a long journey in a life of believing prayer. It is a primer, not a textbook. This is an introductory course; it is not intended to be a graduate-level study. What is written in these pages will get you started praying for your children in a way that brings glory to God and invigorates your own soul.

Of course, I hope whole families can unite around these passages and pray them. I encourage you to include others on your prayer list as you embark on your prayer journey.

Praying the same passage for various people during the week should in no way exhaust the praying we should do each day, but this will help you start on a path that will hopefully last a lifetime. An added benefit is that you'll probably end up memorizing many of the Scripture verses by the time the week is over!

Do you feel unworthy to pray? I have good news for you. Feeling unworthy should never be a reason to stop praying but rather a motivation to pray! Does it matter to the pilot of an airplane whether or not you feel unworthy to fly? Of course not, all that matters is the ticket. Our ticket into the presence of God is the blood of Christ. Just so, our unworthiness is never a barrier to prayer.

God never turns unworthy people away but welcomes them into His presence to teach us what we need to learn.

"Therefore brothers, since we have confidence to enter into the holy places by the blood of Jesus . . . let us draw near with a true heart in full assurance of faith" (Heb. 10:19–23). When we do come to God, it should be with an open spirit of confession and a yielded heart.

Neil Anderson, who is best known for writing and speaking on the topic of spiritual freedom, writes:

> Our children are the most valuable possession God has entrusted to our care. God allows us to enter into only one creative act, and that is procreation. We call them ours but, like everything else we possess, our children belong to God. He knew them from the foundations of the world. We are merely stewards of the precious human lives God has allowed us to bring into the world.[1]

Will you join me in praying for our children, our grandchildren, and others? Let us pray Scripture, echoing back to God His own will. So, "Let us then with confidence draw near to the throne of grace that we may receive mercy and find grace to help in time of need" (Heb. 4:16).

Let us begin by praying for ourselves.

CHAPTER 1

Lord, Change *Me*

Our first prayer as parents should be, "Lord, change *me*!" "Search me, O God, and know my heart! Try me and know my thoughts! And see if there be any grievous way in me, and lead me in the way everlasting!" (Ps. 139:23–24).

One year, for four Wednesday nights at The Moody Church, we announced special prayer meetings that we called POPs (Parents of Prodigals). Not only did we double our prayer meeting attendance, we also had extended times of earnest prayer, with weeping and agonizing before God. We did not see a lot of immediate results, but months and even years later I heard testimonies that God had heard and responded. *We prayed prayers that God is still answering even today!*

Is it always the parent's fault if a child goes astray? No, it is not. I've known many fine and loving parents who have experienced heartache due to children who have left the faith and wandered in the world, experiencing one bitter consequence after another. Divorce, abortion, addiction, and anger have followed them. The father in the parable of the prodigal was not at fault for the rebellion of his younger son. There are some parents who feel guilty, blaming themselves for their child's wrong choices. That is false guilt.

Someone has said, we stand in the presence of two mysteries: the evil of the human heart and the mystery of divine providence. Before Isaac's wife, Rebekah, gave birth to twins, God said, "Yet I have loved Jacob but Esau I have hated" (Mal. 1:2–3). Same mother, same father, but two different destinies.

Often, the choices made by children are not the fault of the parents.

But the interviews at our prayer meetings confirmed that parents often create the environment that spawns the rebellion of their child. So, during those prayer meetings at The Moody Church I would ask, "What is God teaching *you* through your children? And, how might *you* have contributed to their struggles and harmful choices?" Then we would talk about what could be done to redeem the past and pray with hope for the future.

God speaks to us through our children even if they are not rebellious. How vividly I remember, about twenty years ago when I was busy studying the Bible and church history, one of our daughters who was in college said, "Dad, I'm finding it difficult to compete with Martin Luther for time with you!" An arrow right to my heart! A powerful reminder that my priorities were out of whack. Today I am so grateful that our three daughters and our sons-in-law are all walking with God, but I have to admit that as our daughters were growing up, they exposed my selfishness, wrong priorities, and weaknesses.

THE BLESSING OF RECEIVING A BLESSING

Have you blessed your children? In their bestselling book *The Blessing,* Gary Smalley and John Trent explain the emotional baggage that many children carry because they have never had the blessing of their parents. They grow up without the approval and welcome of their parents. Jesus said, "Whoever receives one such child in my name receives me" (Matt. 18:5). But many children are born into homes where they are received in the name of necessity; this is particularly true of children conceived out of wedlock who are perceived as a burden rather than a blessing. Single mothers who are angry with their child's father often overcorrect their children with unacknowledged resentment. The child knows he isn't really wanted; he's seen as a nuisance, not a special treasure who can depend on the acceptance of his parents. Remember, as is often said, whatever we don't forgive, we pass on.

In their book *The Gift of Blessing,* Gary Smalley and John Trent say there are five ways family members, particularly parents, can bless their children:

1. meaningful touch
2. a spoken message
3. attaching high value to the one being blessed
4. picturing a special future for the one being blessed
5. an active commitment to fulfill the blessing[2]

They would agree that if only we were to spend less time *correcting* children and more time *connecting* with them, we would give them an important sense of self-worth and inner fulfillment. There's no substitute for a child being able to delight a parent by sitting on their knees being hugged and enjoyed. Let us commit to giving our children encouragement and the assurance that they are loved and valuable. And, there are more ways than one that the older generation can bless the younger.

I was born into a home where we as children knew that our parents loved us and cared for our well-being. When my father was one hundred years old (he died at 106), Rebecca suggested that I have my father bless me. So with his permission I knelt before him, and he laid his hands on me and prayed an earnest prayer that I will never forget. Let me make this suggestion: if your father is still living and is a Christian, ask him for a special blessing. If not, you might ask an older relative to give you a special blessing. My point is simply this: in an age of the fragmentation of our culture and the breakup of our families, children especially need to feel wanted and valuable. And even older children can receive a special blessing given by some respected adult.

If your child is alive, it is not too late to bless them! Whether at home or away, either directly or with a phone call, give a word of encouragement and hope to your child. Since Jesus is not physically present to bless our children, we are given that privilege. Blessing our children can be one of the ways God fulfills our prayers.

Later, I will suggest a special prayer of blessing for your child.

PARENTS OF PRODIGALS

I believe there are two kinds of parents that often spawn prodigals: parents who are self-righteous, and those who lose their moral authority through their own failures and hypocrisies. Then there are some who have both faults.

Let's talk about the strict, self-righteous parent who believes the key to having good children is by insisting on rigid obedience, high standards, and legalistic rules and regulations. Many times, these expectations are enforced by overcorrection or even abuse. Children in such homes grow up with resentment, often rebelling against the strictness of their parents or church. They long for the day when they can spurn their family, church, and God. Their pent-up anger is waiting to be unleashed.

What's gone wrong? Many parents think that knowledge always results in obedience and that rules motivate the children to develop behavioral patterns that they will follow for the rest of their lives. Of course, knowledge and rules are important, but many legalistic parents neglect a positive emotional connection with their child. They would be wise to heed the mantra of ministry leader and author Josh McDowell: "Rules without relationship leads to rebellion." As we shall see, we are driven not by the mind, but by the heart.

In the early 1970s, a Michigan church was experiencing a revival; its members were repenting of their sins and families were being reconciled to God. One church member returned from a Saturday morning golf game and saw two hundred men on their knees confessing their sins. This latecomer shook his fist and said, "God, you will never get me!"

Why did he say that? Because he had five sons and a hot temper. He later admitted that he frequently over-disciplined his sons, often inconsistently. He knew that if "God got him," he would have to apologize to his sons for how he had wronged them. At that moment, it was a price too high for this proud man who always saw himself as "being right" about everything. But when the conviction of sin was overwhelming, "God got him," and he humbly went to his sons and asked for their forgiveness.

I have discovered that children who are brought up with strict, self-righteous parents are often the hardest to win back to the faith. They are fed up, angry, and are enjoying freedom for the first time. They are not about to be brought again under "the yoke of bondage," which neither they, nor their self-righteous parents, are able to bear.

As a pastor I've often tried to help people see that they have to repent of their self-righteousness. I've learned that it's easier for us to repent of obvious sins than it is to repent of self-righteousness. The self-righteous person is almost incapable of admitting to his sin or guilt. He strives for perfection, believing he's come as close as anyone to attaining that goal. Others have to repent, but he doesn't. He is "right," and that's all that counts. And because he refuses to see himself for what he is, genuine humility is not possible. Nor is repentance that leads to brokenness. The walls of self-protection and denial run deep.

Then there are other children who rebel because one or more of their parents have lost their moral authority due to hypocrisy and failures. A child whose father is unfaithful to the marriage, for example, will grow up with both anger toward the father and resentment toward the mother. Add a divorce into the mix, and you have created an environment in which spiritual rebellion flourishes.

A classic example of this is the Old Testament story of David. David committed the twin sins of adultery and murder, and as a result, lost all moral authority in his family. Absalom, though born into a royal family with a father whose psalms of praise we still read today—*that* son, of *that* famous father, rebelled and died a shameful death.

Let's examine this story more closely.

Absalom had the misfortune of being drop-dead handsome (2 Sam. 14:25–26) with long, luxurious hair and a winning personality. He possessed a natural charm, which posed a temptation he could not resist. Such gifted children have many opportunities to be led astray by their vanity, their godless friends, and their sense of entitlement. They have a sense of pride, and if their expectations are not met, they retaliate with anger and self-justification.

Absalom was even more vulnerable to gross sin because he had no positive emotional connection with his father. When David's hidden sin became public knowledge, he lost his moral authority within the family, and for that matter, within his kingdom. From then on, David was passive, allowing sin to take root in his family without intervention. He still paid attention to the matters of his kingdom, but he neglected his family.

Absalom's anger was not without reason. He had a beautiful sister named Tamar who was sexually violated by his half-brother Amnon. What did their father, David, do about this evil within his family? We read that he was angry, but he did nothing (2 Sam. 13:21). When another of David's sons, Adonijah, plotted to be king in defiance of David's wishes, we read, "His father [David] had never at any time displeased him by asking, 'Why have you done thus and so?'" (1 Kings 1:6). David was morally paralyzed because of his own sin; his lack of moral authority led to moral passivity even in the face of great evil within his family.

In a fit of rage, Absalom kills his half-brother Amnon to avenge what had been done to Tamar. Once Absalom pushed past this moral boundary, it was difficult for him to return to God and back to his father. Guilt, anger, and sexual pleasures drive a child away from God and home. "I hate my father, so I also hate my father's God."

Absalom's goal now was to destroy his father so he could sit on his father's throne. His sense of revenge and entitlement drove him to initiate a rebellion in which he died.

David might have been a great king, but he was a failure as a father.

Here is a lesson for parents.

David did return to God after his sin, and he again experienced the joy of his salvation (Ps. 51:12). Although a father may return to the Lord in repentance, his children might not. David lost four of his sons just as God predicted. Bathsheba's first son died, as did three other sons: Amnon, Absalom, and Adonijah. Unresolved sin on the part of a father can lead to generational sin. Yes, David enjoyed forgiveness and renewed favor with God, but some of his children did not.

Could David have recouped his moral authority? Possibly, if he had not only repented before God but also before his entire family. If he had admitted his shameful sin and requested their forgiveness, he might have reentered into the lives of his children with a sense of humility and honesty. That entrance into the heart of his children might have borne spiritual fruit. But it was not to be.

During those four Wednesday nights at The Moody Church, as I listened to parents' stories of their wayward children, I discovered that in many cases, the rebellious child grew up with a single parent, in a home in which there was divorce, resentment, or addiction. In other cases, the home was strict, where children were expected to obey parents whose authority was to be both respected and unquestioned, homes where abuse was seen as fair discipline.

Every mile children go off the trail is a mile for them to return. Job speaks about those who add "rebellion to their sin" (Job 34:37). But to the brokenhearted parent, I would say, "Don't give up hope!" Let God redeem your story. Rebellious children often do come back to God and to home. Never give up praying! And to the extent that you failed your child, humbly request their forgiveness.

I do not regard myself as a model father, but by God's grace, I have always tried to admit my failures to my children. When she was in her early twenties, our oldest daughter was asked what she liked most about me as her father. How did she answer? Did she say, "I love him because he is the pastor of a well-known church, has a radio program, and writes books?" No.

She replied, "What I appreciated most is that when he was wrong, he admitted it to us; he would ask our forgiveness if he wrongly disciplined us or had acted improperly."

So, as parents, our first prayer should be to ask, "Lord, have I contributed to the problems my child is facing?" When we are totally honest before God, we might be surprised as to what God shows us. After all, there are no perfect parents, no perfect homes, and no perfect children. We must always begin with humility and repentance.

So, before we pray for our children we must ask, how are we as parents doing spiritually? Jim Cymbala, pastor of the Brooklyn Tabernacle, explains what parents must do to prevail in prayer:

> A clear conscience and a pure heart are absolute
> necessities for prevailing prayer. I cannot confidently
> ask God for answers when I cling to the sins that nailed
> His Son to the cross of Calvary. I cannot live in iniquity
> and enjoy the Lord's favor simultaneously. These are
> impossibilities in God's moral universe.[3]

We must begin our prayers for our children with: *"Lord, change me!"*

A PRAYER WE ALL MUST PRAY

Father, You know my faults and failures better than I do. I know I have sometimes failed as a parent through my unacknowledged hypocrisy. Teach me the meaning of deep repentance and transparency in Your presence.

I echo the prayer of David, "Search me, O God, and know my heart! Try me and know my thoughts! And see if there be any grievous way in me, and lead me in the way everlasting!" (Ps. 139:23–24).

As I pray for my child, I pray for myself. Show me not only my failures and sins that have affected my family, but also show me how to restore the past as much as possible. Give me the wisdom I need to reach out to my children, to ask for forgiveness where appropriate, and to extend love where I have withheld it. I claim this promise, "The sacrifices of God are a broken spirit; a broken and a contrite heart, O God, you will not despise" (Ps. 51:17).

Father, I need Your wisdom in the days ahead.

In Jesus' name, Amen.

CHAPTER 2

Lord, Change Their Hearts

Our prayers for our children should not just be asking God for a change of behavior, we should also pray for a change of heart. "Create in me a clean heart, O God, and renew a right spirit within me" (Ps. 51:10).

"Keep your heart with all vigilance, for from it flow the springs of life" (Prov. 4:23).

We must remember that our attitudes and actions grow out of our hearts, not our heads. The heart is the place where our life makes up its mind. By that I mean we make choices according to our desires, not according to carefully reasoned arguments. For the most part, we are controlled, not by the mind's logic or reason, but by the heart's wants and desires. This explains why children who have been homeschooled, and part of a loving family, and have memorized hundreds of verses of Scripture, can still be led astray by their desires (their heart).

A young woman grew up in a Christian home and evangelical church; she even took notes during a class titled "The Bible and the Body," in which the teenagers were given at least a half dozen reasons why premarital sex was wrong. But when she went off to college, she connected with a young Christian man who overwhelmed her with his charm and apparent commitment to Christ. Soon their affection began to blossom and, step-by-step, they ended up becoming more intimate and eventually became sexually active resulting in a pregnancy. Even a course titled "A Hundred Reasons Why Premarital Sex Is Wrong" would not have prevented them from having sex.

Does this mean that our children should not memorize Scripture or take courses such as "The Bible and the Body"? I believe that such information should be mandatory for every child, but if it is not accompanied by a change of heart, it does little good. The heart (the desires) is our decision-maker, not the mind. Passions often trump reason.

Only God can change the heart. Thus, when I pray for our children and grandchildren, I frequently pray, "God, capture their hearts and keep them for Yourself!" We have to pray that God will make them so sensitive to sin that the moment they find themselves headed in the wrong direction, their conscience will trouble them and they will stop, turn around, and run toward Jesus no matter how strong their desires are.

We've already noted that David failed as a father. But early on, he did display a sensitive conscience. In fact, long before he was married, there is an interesting story of when his conscience overruled anger and revenge. He proved that even though we are tempted to act out of our desires, it doesn't have to be so if we have an active conscience. The conscience can keep the heart in check.

David and a hundred of his men entered a cave in an attempt to hide from the vengeful King Saul who was bent on killing David. Then, unexpectedly, Saul entered the same cave to relieve himself, not knowing that David and his men were hiding in the "innermost parts of the cave" (1 Sam. 24:3).

Catch the drama.

The hunter and the hunted were in the same cave! David's men believed that these circumstances were orchestrated by God and this would be David's opportunity to kill this mentally deranged king. They whispered to David that he could eliminate his enemy right now and finally return home, freed from years of harassment. But David would not hear of it; he would not kill his enemy. Instead, he stealthily snuck behind Saul and cut off a corner of his robe.

But later we read that "David's heart struck him" because he had cut off a piece of Saul's robe (1 Sam. 24:5). He felt guilty for doing this small act, for he says, "The Lord forbid that I should do this thing to my lord, the LORD's anointed" (v. 6). David's desire for revenge was restrained by his conscience.

We have to pray that the hearts of our children would be "struck" when they are tempted to sin. If only David's heart would have become "struck" so that he hadn't asked Bathsheba to come over to the palace; if David had listened to his conscience rather than his burning lust, he would have spared himself, his family, and his kingdom years of ongoing grief. As parents, we have to appeal to the conscience of our children; information is not enough, we have to connect with them emotionally and help them develop sensitivity to God.

Your goal as a parent isn't to just try to convince your son that he shouldn't live with his girlfriend. You can do that, of course. You can preach, warn, cajole, and heap guilt on him until he relents, but he probably won't have a genuine change of heart. And we all know that the deeper a person goes into sin, the more irrational he becomes. So what should a parent's goal be?

A child who has chosen to live immorally doesn't just need a change of friends and relationships, he needs a change of heart. God has to make him so miserable in his sin that the misery of breaking up with his live-in girlfriend is more tolerable than the misery of offending a God he is commanded to love. It's all about the heart. It's not just about training the mind but heightening the sensitivity of the conscience.

One of the best examples in the Bible about resisting sexual sin is found in the life of Joseph. You know the story: Joseph was young, handsome and single. We read "Now Joseph was handsome in form and appearance. And after a time his master's wife cast her eyes on Joseph and said, 'Lie with me!'" (Gen. 39:6–7). He and Potiphar's wife worked in the house together all day and she was strongly attracted to him, and urged him to have sex with her. Her advances were not just occasional, but repeated. We read, "And as she spoke to Joseph day after day, he would not listen to her, to lie beside her or to be with her" (v. 10).

Think of all the rationalizations Joseph might have used: he was single, away from home, her husband trusted him, and what is more, they could arm themselves with a pack of lies and feel exonerated if an accusation was made. But Joseph did not do that. His response should be engraved on the hearts of all of our children, "How then can I do this great wickedness and sin against God?" (v. 9).

Two truths kept Joseph from contaminating his soul: first, he had a right view of sin. He did not call adultery an "affair" or otherwise tried to lessen the gravity of the sin. Second, he had a right view of God. Joseph's family was not there; he was alone without relatives in Egypt, but God was with him. If he committed this sin, the God he loved would be grieved. The greatest deterrent against sexual sin is a love for God that is greater than our love of sin.

Of course, God can also forgive and restore those who

have fallen into sexual sin. Sixteen centuries ago, a Christian mother named Monica had two sons. She was in an arranged marriage; she was married to a man who cared nothing for the Christian faith. Nevertheless, one son followed the Lord, while the other child was intrigued with pagan philosophy and had a child with his mistress. For seventeen years, Monica prayed with no evident answer to her prayers. She asked her bishop why God had not answered, and he encouraged her, "It is not possible that the son of these tears should perish."[4]

And her son was saved! While in a garden, he overheard a child say, "Pick up and read," and Monica's son arbitrarily opened the Bible to Romans 13:12–14: "The night is far gone; the day is at hand. So then let us cast off the works of darkness and put on the armor of light. Let us walk properly as in the daytime, not in orgies and drunkenness, not in sexual immorality and sensuality, not in quarreling and jealousy. But put on the Lord Jesus Christ, and make no provision for the flesh, to gratify its desires."

Monica's son was converted. He was the theologian/philosopher and writer Augustine of Hippo, who has had a great influence in the Christian church. In his *Confessions,* he said that his mother's tears "watered the ground under her eyes in every place where she prayed"[5] for him. Seventeen years of praying brought results.

After he was converted, Augustine's mistress wanted to continue their sinful relationship. Apparently she ran after him as he walked along the street and shouted, "It is I!" But he replied, "But it is not I!" God transformed his heart, and along with that came a change of behavior.

You and I cannot change the hearts of our children. Nor can we convert them. Only God can do that, and that is why we pray so earnestly for them and turn them over to God. There comes a time when we have to stop our attempts to change our child's behavior and let God do what only He can do. We cannot do God's work for Him.

Yes, there have been times when praying parents have not lived to see the answer to their prayers. My experience has been that not all prayed-for children turn to God. But I've also seen some miracles where children turned to God near the end of their lives—a testament that God answered the prayers of their parents—parents who would not take *no* for an answer.

Although there are no guarantees, I want to encourage you with the words the bishop spoke to Augustine's mother: "Only pray God for him . . ." And then, like Monica, pray without ceasing: *"Lord, change their hearts!"*[6]

A PRAYER WE ALL MUST PRAY

Father, capture the heart of my child and keep it for Yourself. I pray, first and foremost, that my child might be genuinely converted; create in them a new heart and a desire for a clean heart. When he or she has the opportunity to sin, may they not have the desire; when they have the desire, may they not have the opportunity.

Where sin has gotten a strong hold on them, break that obsessive power; reveal the consequences of sin and show them that Your way is best. Give them a heart of repentance; may their hearts be grieved when they grieve Your Spirit. Teach them that "The fear of the Lord is the beginning of knowledge [wisdom] but fools despise wisdom and instruction" (Prov. 1:7).

Father, I turn my child over to You; O Lord, do what I cannot. May I not look at what I see, but rather look at what I know You can do. Therefore, rather than fixing my eyes on my child, I fix my eyes on You. Show me the promises I must believe in order to rest in Your grace and strength.

In Jesus' name, Amen.

CHAPTER 3

Lord, Let Sin Become Bitter, So Grace May Become Sweet

"There is severe discipline for him who forsakes the way; whoever hates reproof will die" (Prov. 15:10).

"It is for discipline that you have to endure. God is treating you as sons. For what son is there whom his father does not discipline?" (Heb. 12:7).

The story of the prodigal son is instructive. You've heard his story many times, but he always has more to teach us. This young man, from a great family with a wonderful father, looked at the world and thought he had been shortchanged! He was intrigued by the lure of the world: the lust of the flesh, the lust of the eyes, and the pride of life. He probably had good instruction, but his heart drew him to the "far country" (see Luke 15:11–32).

What a thankless son! At least he could have waited until his father died before he received his inheritance; but he went to his father and said in effect, "I can't even wait until you die. Give me my inheritance now!" Those two little words "give me" are words of entitlement. "I have it coming to me. I *deserve* this."

So the father, according to the laws of the Old Testament, gave him one-third, and the elder brother two-thirds.

Wordless—because he knew what the far country was like—the father watched his son go down. The father understood that the far country made promises it couldn't keep. The father knew that in the far country, all the wells were dry. But interestingly, he didn't try to talk the son out of going. There comes a time in the life of a child when he has to make his own decisions. And so, heartbroken and grieved, the father watched his son leave.

The boy traveled as far away as possible. "I want to go where nobody knows me, where I don't have any relatives or friends or an elder brother looking over my shoulder and telling me, 'You shouldn't be doing this.'" Today, children might say, "I want to go to New York. I want to go to Chicago. I want to go to Los Angeles—as far away as I can get from home so I have no accountability to my family."

Then the prodigal misused the blessings his father gave him by spending his inheritance on riotous, reckless living. He used his money for sins that his father abhorred. And he enjoyed it.

But his money ran out. And with that, his friends left him. "And he was longing to be fed with the pods that the pigs ate, and no one gave him anything. But when he came to himself, he said . . ." (Luke 15:16–17).

But when he came to himself!

The pigsty did its work. It was the pigsty and not the father's love that made him return home. And the father was pleased to welcome him home. Sometimes the pigsty is the motivation a child needs to return home and return to God. In at least two instances that I am personally aware of, it was a prison sentence that God used to get a wayward child's attention. For others it was a broken marriage, an addiction, or an economic meltdown. We all know that those entangled in one consequence of sin or another often have to reach bottom before they honestly seek help. There is power in desperation.

I've known parents who have circumvented the work of the pigsty. They have repeatedly bailed a child out of jail, or in one way or another spent a great deal of effort and money trying to lessen the consequences of their child's rebellion. They are enablers who pay the debts of their wayward children; they intervene in the courts, and they repeatedly come to their child's rescue.

I know a dear woman, now in heaven, who was a model enabler of her adult, alcoholic son. Year after year, she paid his rent, gave him money for groceries, and enough spending money to continue his drinking. All the while, she prayed for him earnestly, regularly, and with faith that he would repent and turn his life over to Christ, and that she would see him in heaven. When he was in his fifties, she died without seeing him repent. I believe that her prayers will yet be answered even though she provided the crutch her adult son needed to keep living without changing his ways.

When some of us suggested that she needed to stop supporting him, she wouldn't hear of it. He was her son, and she would pay his debts even though he didn't find work or find a way of supporting himself. She simply would not abandon giving him his monthly money supply; therefore, he saw no reason to deal with his laziness and alcoholism.

I understand this mother.

The heart of a parent is such that it is difficult to watch any child, even a grown man, live on the streets or end up in jail. However, some of us thought that it would have been best if she continued to assure him of her unconditional love while letting him know that he had to find his own way in the world. As the prodigal ran away from home, his father didn't go looking for him and buy him lunch. He let sin run its course.

To put it clearly: give your child to God and trust Him to do what you and I cannot. The pigsty might be your child's only hope. Pray that sin's bitterness will not be sweetened by well-meaning relatives or friends. Grace is never sweet unless sin is bitter.

And please, when they return home, welcome your child home with open arms! Unconditional love is more powerful than lectures, arguments, and incrimination. If the child needs discipline, give it, but always keep the candle burning in your window. Our children need to know that there is one place on earth where they will be loved simply because they are a son or daughter.

Rebecca and I are intimately acquainted with a family whose son, Felix, was rebellious, angry, and determined to go his own way. He began by smoking pot and from there went on to using cocaine and ecstasy, eventually selling the drugs to make enough money to cover his own addiction. He was arrested three times, and because he violated his probation, he was incarcerated twice.

He said that while he was in prison, all of his thoughts were selfish—he asked himself why he was caught and what he could do better next time. He had no real remorse or repentance. His life was filled with lies and deceit—and anger.

When he was released, he went back to his former lifestyle. He was frustrated and depressed. When his mother encouraged him to come to church with the family, he said no because he felt so "unclean and ashamed." On the occasions when he did come for Christmas or Easter, he would leave and "get high" to deaden the conviction and pain.

One day it all came to a head. Four of his close friends moved away, so he felt isolated, alone—and depressed. When his car was broken into and towed, that was the last straw. He lashed out at God. Sweating with heart palpitations he shouted, "Why are You doing this to me?" He angrily asked God what he had done to deserve this.

Then he heard a voice within him saying, "It's not Me, it's you. It's your sins, and if you continue down this path, it will lead to death." Then he heard, "Just confess your sins to Me!"

With that, Felix began to confess his sins; the Holy Spirit brought to his remembrance evils he had long since forgotten. Words of repentance poured out of his mouth. He told God that he was willing to part with anything—anything that stood in the way of fellowship with the Almighty. He asked God to free him from harmful friends, from addictions, and from depression and anger. After an hour of heartfelt brokenness, he felt free; he was a new man. In his words, "The next morning as the sun streamed through my window, it was as if all of my ugly past was gone—forever." His longings changed radically; there was no more desire for drugs, deceit, and anger. Instead, he found a hunger for God's Word and a desire to fellowship with God's people.

His parents were pleasantly surprised when he asked if he could attend church with them the following Sunday. They had prayed, fasted, and believed, but they didn't know God would do something so dramatic. Sometimes God does "far more abundantly than all that we ask or think" (Eph. 3:20).

Today, you would not recognize the young man we once knew. He is involved in ministry, has a burden for missions, and gives praise to God in every circumstance.

The pigsty had done its work. What reason cannot teach a child, the consequences of sin can. Sin can only be seen for what it is when the Holy Spirit shows us its true nature.

Let us pray that sin will be so bitter that grace—the undeserved matchless grace of God—will be seen as sweet.

A PRAYER WE ALL MUST PRAY

Father, show my child the end result of a worldly life. Keep him from thinking that he knows better than You how to run his life. Use whatever means necessary for my child to admit their need. Let the pigsty do its work.

Father, I cry to You in desperation. Do what I cannot. Do what no man can and show my child that Your way is best. Use guilt, disappointment, and heartache to bring them submissively into Your care.

Show him that in the world, all the wells are dry—the world's nourishment becomes nauseating and its promises are never kept. Lord, teach him the beauty of the Father's home. Draw him to Yourself.

Today I bring to this prayer the victory of Jesus who died, was buried, and ascended into heaven, having won a victory over all principalities and powers and every name that is named in this world and in the world to come.

In Jesus' name, Amen.

CHAPTER 4

Lord, I Refuse to Let Satan Have My Child

For we do not wrestle against flesh and blood, but against the rulers, against the authorities, against the cosmic powers over this present darkness, against the spiritual forces of evil in the heavenly places" (Eph. 6:12).

There is an invisible, spiritual world in which there is conflict between good and evil, between God and the devil. We are all influenced by the outcome of these battles. Many Christians know very little about spiritual warfare, and they may even be fearful of learning about it.

In the New Testament, we find the story of a woman who simply would not let Satan have her child. It's a story that should stimulate all of us to greater intercession, greater faith, and tenacity in our prayer life. This unnamed woman needed help for her demonized child, and she would not give up until she got it!

In brief, here is her story:

> And Jesus went away from there and withdrew to the district of Tyre and Sidon. And behold, a Canaanite woman from that region came out and was crying, "Have mercy on me, O Lord, Son of David; my daughter is severely oppressed by a demon." But he did not answer her a word. And his disciples came and begged him, saying, "Send her away, for she is crying out after us." He answered, "I was sent only to the lost sheep of the house of Israel." But she came and knelt before him, saying, "Lord, help me." And he answered, "It is not right to take the children's bread and throw it to the dogs." She said, "Yes, Lord, yet even the dogs eat the crumbs that fall from their masters' table." Then Jesus answered her, "O woman, great is your faith! Be it done for you as you desire." And her daughter was healed instantly. (Matt. 15:21–28)

We have no idea how this woman learned about Jesus. Rumors about His miraculous powers evidently reached her somehow, and when she heard that He was coming to her area, she knew that this was her moment of opportunity. She already knew the important facts about Him and even called Him the Son of David!

We can't be sure exactly why her daughter had a demon, but we do know that demonic spirits can run in family lines, especially among those who are followers of false religions or those who explicitly worship idols. Tyre and Sidon were Gentile cities steeped in Baal worship. So, it should not be surprising that a child born to parents who almost certainly worshiped pagan idols would have a demonic affliction. Again, I must point out that the mother had more spiritual insight than many Christians today, because she was able to recognize the difference between a child who simply misbehaved and the actual activity of an evil spirit.

This dear woman—God bless her—would not find it easy to get the help from Jesus that she desired. But she refused to be deterred. No matter the barriers, she was determined to not take no for an answer. You and I can learn from her example!

Let us consider the barriers that she overcame in getting to Jesus so that her child could be healed.

First, she had to break through the *religious* barrier. Those who are brought up in false religions worshiping false gods find it difficult to leave, often because of opposition from their families. She could have said, "I was brought up worshiping Baal, and I will die worshiping Baal." But she was willing to stand against her culture's religious expectations to get help for her daughter.

Second, she not only had to reject her religion but her

culture as well. The Jews famously hated Gentiles, so the thought of a Gentile going to a Jew for help was unthinkable. Let's reverse the situation: it would be like a Jewish person today asking a Palestinian for help. Humiliating. Shaming.

The fact that she was a woman made the situation even more culturally reprehensible. It's not just that she was a Gentile going to Jews for help, but the idea that a Gentile woman would go to a Jewish man for help was a cause for shaming. Yet this mother did not care what her culture taught or what the neighbors or her family thought. She was desperate, and a desperate situation called for a desperate action. Let the neighbors wag their heads; let the religious leaders ostracize her. Her daughter was demonized, and she would get help.

Third, she had to contend with a *divided home.* Where was the father of this child? We don't know. He might have been working; he might have been dead. Be that as it may, the fact is that this mother had to play the role of the father. She needed help, and if there was no father around, she would step into his shoes!

I expect that many single mothers will read this book—I want you to be encouraged. There are times when you will have to play the role of father as well as mother. You may have to become an advocate for your child because your husband has, for whatever reason, abdicated his responsibility to provide spiritual leadership for you and your children. You may be divorced, or an unmarried mother, or widowed. Whatever the case may be, this mother's story offers you hope. Stand up for your children without wavering.

The fourth barrier this mother had to overcome was the *silence* of Jesus. Despite her pleas, we read, "He did not answer her a word." That seems insulting to us. When she gets to the One she knew could help, she gets the silent treatment; He turns a deaf ear.

Are you, as a parent, put off by the silence of God? Are you weary of crying up to God and not receiving an answer? Let us remember that the silence of God should not be interpreted as the indifference of God. Jesus was silent, but He was not unconcerned. Even in His silence, He was plotting mercy. Someone has well said that "a teacher is silent during an exam!"

This woman would not be put off by Jesus' silence, and her challenges continued.

The next obstacle she had to overcome was the *rejection* of the disciples. The twelve were annoyed by this persistent woman who didn't have the good sense to leave them alone. If you were this woman, how would you like to have heard them say, "Send her away, for she is crying out after us." The text says they actually *begged* Jesus to have her sent away!

You might be surprised at the number of people who have left the Christian faith because of the Lord's disciples. God's people are often a stumbling block that stands between Jesus and His would-be followers. Too often, disciples are more of a hindrance than a help in getting people to Jesus.

But this rejected woman would not take the spite emanating from the disciples as a reason to stop her pleading. Others might turn away, but she would not.

And the most difficult barriers were still to come.

Jesus makes what, to us at first glance, might seem to be two racially charged statements.

"I was sent only to the lost sheep of the house of Israel" (Matt. 15:24). That was true, of course. Jesus was sent as Israel's Messiah, and He even requested that His disciples go only "to the lost sheep of the house of Israel." Of course, His larger intention was that through the "house of Israel" the entire world be reached with the gospel. But on earth, His mission was largely limited to the nation of Israel.

Even this rebuke was not enough to stop this mother's pleadings. She knelt before Jesus and cried simply, "Lord, help me!"

And then comes this bombshell.

Jesus has an even more stinging rebuke, "It is not right to take the children's bread and throw it to the dogs!"

Ouch!

The Jews called the Gentiles "dogs." The word they used did not refer to house puppies, but to scavenger dogs that roamed the streets eating whatever they could. Was Jesus using a racially charged slur?

Not so.

This remark was not racist for two reasons. First, the word for *dog* Jesus used here was not the one used for scrawny scavengers (as when the Jews wanted to demean Gentiles), but rather, it was a term denoting small dogs or puppies; it was the word for household pets. Clearly, Jesus' rebuke was not as harsh as it appears. As William Barclay wrote, "We can be quite sure that the smile on Jesus' face and the compassion in his eyes robbed the words of all insult and bitterness."[7] Most probably, Jesus' tone and attitude told the real story of His care and desire to help.

Second, I believe this was a test of this woman's faith. I have no doubt that the reason He went north through Tyre and Sidon was almost certainly for the benefit of this woman. He left the boundaries of His own land with her in mind.

Even as He said these words, He was planning mercy.

The answer this woman gave brings tears to my eyes.

"Yes, Lord, yet even the dogs eat the crumbs that fall from their masters' table."

In effect, what she was saying is this: "By all means feed the children first. Let them eat their fill. I want nothing taken from them; I want only a few crumbs that fall from the table—a few crumbs that they would never miss!"

What is Jesus going to do with a woman like that?

"'O woman, great is your faith! Be it done for you as you desire.' And her daughter was healed instantly" (v. 28).

The demon had met his match! At the word of Jesus, that evil spirit had to flee. Deliverance came because a desperate woman would not take no for an answer.

SPIRITUAL WARFARE

When we read in Scripture that we do not wrestle against flesh and blood but against cosmic powers of darkness, do we really believe what we are reading?

I am convinced that it is not possible to break the bondages of addiction, the passions of rage, or the obsessions with worldly priorities without encountering direct conflict with forces of evil. Let's take Paul's words literally: we are in continual combat with unseen evil forces.

It is not my intention to discuss the oft-asked question as to whether a Christian can be demon possessed; certainly, if possession means ownership, the answer is no. But I believe that Christians can be harassed, controlled, and even invaded by evil spirits that often need to be confronted. I heard a testimony from a former heroin addict who, thanks to the fervent prayer of Christians, was delivered from evil spirits who left his body. Years later, he is still serving the Lord with no relapses.

I do not mean to say that all addicts can be instantly delivered by praying Christians who know how to confront spirits. Every case is different, every story of deliverance has its own nuances, but it is not possible to be free from angry inner voices and obsessive urges without recognizing that we are battling more than the eye can see.

As parents, we do well to pray prayers that confront the enemy who is seeking to destroy our children. This is not a time for casual prayers or thoughtless petitions. It is a time of "wrestling," of earnest pleading, and insisting that the devil not have our child.

We are all at war with Satan, whether we realize it or not. There are forces in the spiritual world that are doing all they can to destroy families. There are "strongholds" that cannot be defeated by new resolutions to do better, nor by trying to reason with those who are irrational, angry, and driven. When we pray for our children, we cannot look at what we see but rather what is unseen, and continue to believe that God will use our prayers. Remember, it is not just their faith that is being tested; ours as parents is also being tested.

In her book *Satan, You Can't Have My Children,* Iris Delgado writes, "A Christian parent needs to remember that the battle must be waged against the devil and demonic forces, and not against the person who is behaving in an ungodly manner."[8] Of course we must confront the person who is acting in an ungodly manner, but we do so knowing that there is also an invisible war that seeks to perpetuate evil.

When we pray, we stand with unwavering conviction on the promise that Jesus has won a decisive victory over the powers of darkness. "He disarmed the rulers and authorities and put them to open shame, by triumphing over them in him" (Col. 2:15).

How will the saints remain faithful during the tribulation when evil is unleashed worldwide under the rule of antichrist and his minions? We read, "And they have conquered him by the blood of the Lamb and by the word of their testimony, for they loved not their lives even unto death" (Rev. 12:11).

If you are a born again Christian, you are a threat to Satan! In fact, a pastor who counsels those who are harassed by evil spirits often reminds them that Satan is more afraid of them than they ever need be of him. Satan knows you're united with the victorious Christ seated in the heavenlies. If we disbelieve or are intimidated, Satan is relieved; if we know who we are and know where we stand, we can pray no matter what the circumstances.

Delgado tells us how she prays for her children: "I pray in faith, trusting God to intervene in their lives. I refuse to be moved by what I see, hear or feel . . . then I can enter spiritual warfare and praying scriptures."[9]

Blessed are those parents who do not fear the attacks of Satan but pray confidently, appealing to the victory of Christ who "disarmed the rulers and authorities and put them to open shame, by triumphing over them in him" (Col. 2:15). As E. M. Bounds wrote, "We can do nothing without prayer . . . It surmounts or removes all obstacles, overcomes every resisting force and gains its ends in the face of invincible hindrances."[10]

BREAKING THE INFLUENCE
OF THE SINS OF THE PARENTS

Sadly, that is not the only story in the New Testament about a child having a demonic spirit. Read this carefully about a father seeking help for his son: "And behold, a spirit seizes him, and he suddenly cries out. It convulses him so that he foams at the mouth, and shatters him, and will hardly leave him. And I begged your disciples to cast it out, but they could not" (Luke 9:39–40). Jesus immediately rebuked the spirit and the boy was healed. In Matthew's account of the same story, the disciples asked Jesus why they could not cast it out and Jesus answered, "Because of your little faith" (Matt. 17:20).

How do such children inherit a demonic spirit?

When God gave the Ten Commandments, He forbade idolatry and then added these words, "for I the Lord your God am a jealous God, visiting the iniquity of the fathers on the children to the third and the fourth generation of those who hate me, but showing steadfast love to thousands of those who love me and keep my commandments" (Ex. 20:5–6).

Let's try to unpack this important issue.

First, keep in mind that this Scripture is often proven true simply because children have a natural tendency to follow in their father's footsteps. Frequently we see alcoholism running in families; the father is an alcoholic and his son or daughter follows suit. However, this cycle is not inevitable. We must help children see that they might have grown up with a victimhood mentality, but the family of God gives them a new identity.

Second, note that this judgment against sin is applicable only to those who "hate" God. When a person is born again by the Holy Spirit, any such curses can be broken, because that person is under new ownership. There are plenty of examples of children born into evil homes who have defied the odds and have, through Christ's power, lived lives that honor God and are a tribute to His grace. As the Canaanite mother proved, the evil influence of idolatry can be broken through the power of Christ.

Third, it's worth noting God says elsewhere that He will hold the children responsible for their own sins, not the sins of their parents (Deut. 24:16; Ez. 18:20).

To what extent are the iniquities of the father "visited upon the children"? There might well be generational spirits who concentrate on various family lines, exploiting the weaknesses of the offspring of idolatrous parents. But the balancing fact is that there are all kinds of spiritually minded Christians who grew up in abusive, hateful, and idolatrous families. Such a curse can only have control over believers if we think we must be subject to it. I like to remind people that Satan has only as much power over us as we allow him to have!

Over the years, I have talked with fine Christians who have feared that curses have been put upon them by people who sought their destruction. I pointed out that if it were so, Satan would have had to go to God and ask permission to touch them. Curse or no curse, the fact is that the lives of Christians are not in the hands of Satan but in the hands of the Lord. Satan is paralyzed, unable to touch us unless God allows it.

Jesus, speaking to Peter who would soon betray Him, said, "Simon, Simon, behold, Satan demanded to have you, that he might sift you like wheat, but I have prayed for you that your faith may not fail. And when you have turned again, strengthen your brothers" (Luke 22:31–32). Satan was not permitted to bypass Jesus to get to Peter. He had to get the permission of Jesus first.

Satan, I am convinced, wants us to think of him differently. He wants us to believe that he has independent power. If that is our understanding, we are caught off guard, filled with fear that the enemy of our souls might be acting when God isn't even watching! Or at least, we might think, God has given Satan independent powers that are unreported and unsupervised. But Satan has to stay within the parameters God gives him.

One woman, who was the victim of occult/sexual abuse,

became a Christian and was saved out of a life of horrid memories of childhood terror. She feared a curse had been placed upon her, an oath that she was to die at the age of forty-six, the age at which her satanic father died. When it dawned on her that Satan could not act independently of God, when she understood that Satan could not afflict her unless God willed it, her fearful heart was at rest. Even if God did give Satan permission to strike her down at the age of forty-six, she felt assured she would die within the will of God, held in His grasp. (She has lived well past that age!)

Who do we think Satan is, if we think that he, not God, determines the day of our death? Let it be clearly affirmed: our lives are not in Satan's hands, but in God's hands. Satan cannot act apart from divine providence. Death need not terrify us. Christ, not the devil, said, "Fear not, I am the first and the last, and the living one. I died, and behold I am alive forevermore, and I have the keys of Death and Hades" (Rev. 1:17–18).

I've met Christians who have been paralyzed in their Christian life because there was occultism (and therefore idolatry) in their family line. Some think they must live the rest of their lives under a cloud, a curse that will follow them until they die. One Christian man told me that his children and grandchildren would have to live without the full blessing of God because there were no Christians in his family going back to the third and fourth generation. But in Christ, such cycles are broken. All believers are entitled to the same blessings from God who has "blessed us in Christ with every spiritual blessing in heavenly places" (Eph. 1:3).

No matter your family history, believers are not under a curse—for Christ bore our curse. The transformation from the kingdom of darkness into the kingdom of light is complete. Satan wants us to be preoccupied with his control, his curses, his "unavoidable schemes." But like Pilate of old, he has no power against us except that which is given him from above.

Throughout the years, I've had parents tell me that their child thinks he or she is being visited by an unseen friend who tells them that he will lead them and protect them. One parent told me that his young son had a "friend" who said "God hates you, but I can help you." So the boy called on this "friend" in times of trouble not realizing it was an evil spirit.

When the parents learned more about this strange friendship, they rebuked the demon in the name of Christ. Of course there was a battle, but the demon was routed, for one good reason: these parents knew what some people do not, namely that demons have no such rights to haunt a child.

Although we don't know why this child was affected in this way, we know that the parents put on the full armor of God and were able to stand against the schemes of the devil (Eph. 6:10–12). Think of what the parents learned about the power of God, and what the child learned about the love of Christ for him and the deceptive nature of evil. Like Peter who fell for Satan's wiles but then strengthened his brothers, so this family is the better for the experience. Satan chose a battlefield and lost.

Martin Luther had a servant who lived in despair because she had "sold her soul to the devil." Luther answered her by asking, "What if you were to write a bill of sale, agreeing to sell one of my children as a slave. Would that agreement have any value?"

"No, of course not, I have no right to sell your child who doesn't belong to me!"

To which Luther, in effect, replied, "You are one of God's children, and since He owns your soul, it cannot be given away to another." Those who belong to Christ's kingdom can never be bound by an agreement to a king who has no rights to them. Thus, by definition, all agreements and oaths made by a child of God to the devil are null and void the moment they are made.

As parents, we have all taken our children to the zoo, and as we have walked past the lion's cage, the children become frightened, but we don't. Why? Because children usually look at the lion, while we look at the bars.

Satan is a roaring lion, seeking whom he may devour (1 Peter 5:8). Apparently, he roars to frighten us; he stalks and plots against us. But just like the lion in the zoo, he is only free within the parameters of his cage. He roams only where God permits. This does not mean that he has already been bound in the abyss—that is a future event. Today he is allowed to wander and damage non-Christians as well as Christians, but he does so only under God's watchful eye. His sentence has already been pronounced and his eternal doom a fixed reality, but for now he is out on bail. Yet, God draws the line and says, "This far and no farther." He must stay behind the bars God has ordained.

Let me encourage you by another story of answered prayer.

If you are a baseball fan, you have probably heard of Darryl Strawberry. He was a slugger who graced several covers of *Sports Illustrated* and helped the Mets and the Yankees win World Series championships.

But off the field his life was driven by cocaine, alcohol, and sex addictions. Despite his prowess on the baseball field, he was lonely and empty. Two failed marriages, jail time, and bankruptcy are the messes he was in. But looking back, he is glad that he struck out in life.

Despite his dysfunctional childhood marred by an abusive, alcoholic father, he had a Christian mother who prayed for him. Today he likens God's faithfulness in his life to that of Job in the Old Testament. In an article that appeared in *Decision Magazine*, he was quoted as saying,

> God let me see the fame, the fortune, the brokenness,
> the emptiness, almost left for dead but He stepped in
> the middle and said, "Satan, OK, that's enough. You can
> torment him all you want, but at the end, his soul belongs

to Me and I'm going to take him, and I'm going to use him for My glory."[11]

Eventually, through attending a Billy Graham crusade, he accepted Christ as his Savior. His struggles continued, but after attending Narcotics Anonymous he was freed from his addictions and today he and his wife, Tracy, hold seminars, giving help and direction to needy couples looking for hope. Strawberry Ministries is dedicated to sharing their story and preaching the gospel.

Strawberry credits his mom as a prayer warrior who refused to give up on him. After she died of breast cancer twenty years ago, he found her prayer journal under her bed with this entry, "'God, knock him off his throne; whatever You do, save him.'"[12]

Like the Canaanite woman, Strawberry's mother refused to give up until Satan had to back off at the command of God.

You may be a single parent, or perhaps you have been divorced, or you live with an unbeliever in your home. Regardless, exercise the privilege of prayer that all believers enjoy. If the Canaanite mother were here, she would urge us to pray fervently and not take no for an answer!

"Lord, I refuse to let Satan have my child!"

A PRAYER WE ALL MUST PRAY

Lord God, I thank You that You reign in heaven and on earth. Thank You that Jesus defeated Satan, and the wiles of the evil one have been revealed in Your Word so that we do not have to be ignorant of his evil designs. Today I open my heart to You about the brokenness in my own life and in the life of my child. I rejoice that Your presence is as much with me now as when Jesus was here on earth and proclaimed victory to the captives and set people free. I thank You that the demons had to obey when You told them, "Come out of the man, you unclean spirit" (Mark 5:8). I rejoice that moment by moment Satan and his demons are subject to Your authority.

Father, I pray that I might rely on Your promise, "Submit yourselves therefore to God. Resist the devil and he will flee from you. Draw near to God, and he will draw near to you" (James 4:7–8). Show me the areas in my life where I have not yet submitted to Your authority; my desire is that I might withhold nothing, but might recognize Your total ownership of my life and all that I have, including my child.

On the basis of Your power and victory, I rebuke any and all demonic spirits who trouble my child. I will persist in my prayer; I will also persist in giving You praise for the victory already won. Because of Your triumph, I refuse to let Satan have my child!

In the strong name of Jesus, my Lord, Amen.

Let's Start Praying

Now we turn to the God-honoring practice of praying Scripture. It is important that we pray those Scriptures that apply to us as New Testament followers of Christ. Some of the prayers and promises in the Old Testament that refer to the material blessings of God for Israel do not apply directly to the church. Many so-called prosperity preachers, failing to understand this distinction, insist that you can give your way to prosperity because God promised the blessings of good crops and fruit to His people if they brought their full "tithe into the storehouse" (Mal. 3:10–12). But of course, Old Testament blessings about God's presence and spiritual blessings may be claimed by us. Yes, of course we can pray for material blessings and physical healings, but we have no guarantee that those prayers will be answered as prayed.

The psalms, which are so filled with praise and worship, can indeed be one of the most blessed sections of Scripture to pray. In the New Testament, we have the prayers of Jesus and Paul that can be prayed by us knowing that they "teach us to pray."

My plea is simply that we exercise discernment. My own prayers often grow out of my daily Scripture readings. Ask for wisdom and God will give it to you (James 1:5).

A PRAYER TO BEGIN YOUR DAY

A number of years ago, at the suggestion of a fellow pastor, I began the practice of praying a brief prayer even before I get out of bed in the morning. It is simply, "O God, glorify Yourself in my life today at my expense!" Then I also pray a different scriptural prayer for one of my children and at least one grandchild.

More recently, I have begun this initial prayer time by quoting Isaiah 60:1, "Arise, shine for your light has come, and the glory of the LORD has risen upon you." We need to be reminded that life is not about us, but about God and His glory; it is about shining His light into this dark world. So I pray two prayers: that I might shine a light and also live for God's glory. I've shared this practice with our children and grandchildren and hope this motivation for God's glory becomes theirs as well.

After I shared this at a gathering, one man took me into his office and showed me a small colorful prayer rug hanging on the wall. He took it down and said he was taking it home and every morning as soon as he got out of bed he determined he would kneel on this rug and pray the prayer I suggested. This is a reminder that each of us has to have the freedom to begin our prayer time however we wish, as long as God and His glory is on our minds as we begin the day ahead.

Later in the day, once I have begun my routine of Scripture reading, I have a more extended time of prayer for my family and grandchildren along with other requests. Don't let the brief prayer before you get out of bed be a substitute for a more focused time of fellowship with God.

If you have not been praying Scripture before, I think this practice will revolutionize your prayer time. The following are prayers for each day of the week, but by no means are they exhaustive: you can choose your own passages of Scripture to pray. These daily prayers illustrate praying Scripture for our children. During your Bible reading, look for verses to pray.

MONDAY: A PRAYER OF BLESSING
FOR OUR CHILDREN

"'Let the children come to me; do not hinder them,
for to such belongs the kingdom of God. Truly, I say
to you, whoever does not receive the kingdom of God
like a child shall not enter it.' And he took them in his
arms and blessed them, laying his hands on them"
(Mark 10:14–16).

I've often tried to imagine this scene. Jesus with children on His lap, holding them in His arms with tenderness and prayerful attention. Imagine, receiving a blessing from Jesus!

Jesus is not with us in the flesh today as He was back then. Who is going to bless our children? The answer, of course, is that parents and grandparents play that role, and we do so with joy and a positive spirit.

Jesus taught that we should receive children in His name (Matt. 18:5). I want to repeat what I have already referred to: many children today are received into homes in the name of necessity. I think of the many unwanted, unborn children whose parents are angry, resentful, and filled with revenge. Such a child usually does not have the blessing of his parents and grows up without the acceptance and affection every child should receive.

Angry fathers accept their children only on a performance basis. But the boy is never good enough; the daughter is always an annoyance. Where there should be joy and encouragement, there is resentment and latent anger. Add to that a narcissistic parent who is unable to feel the pain they are causing their child and you have the formula for future insecurity, rebellion, and a futile search for meaning—a search that will lead to poor choices and spiritual emptiness.

We must bless our children. They need to know that they have our unconditional love. And instead of concentrating on their faults and missteps, we need to affirm the good and encourage signs of respect and hope.

With the example of Jesus in our minds, let's pray a blessing over our children.

Let Us Pray

Father, forgive me for often pointing out the faults in my child and not encouraging that which is good and hopeful. I pray this prayer of Moses for my child:

"The LORD bless you and keep you; the LORD make his face to shine upon you and be gracious to you; the LORD lift up his countenance upon you and give you peace" (Num. 6:24–26).

I thank You that You told Moses that with this prayer he could put "your name on the people of Israel" (v. 27) and they would be blessed. And so I put Your name upon my children.

Thank You, Father, for this opportunity to pray for this special blessing upon my children.

In Jesus' name, Amen.

TUESDAY: A PRAYER TO KEEP OUR CHILDREN FROM EVIL

"I do not ask that you take them out of the world, but that you keep them from the evil one. They are not of the world, just as I am not of the world. Sanctify them in the truth; your word is truth. And for their sake I consecrate myself, that they also may be sanctified in truth" (John 17:15–17, 19).

Many parents who bolt their doors at night nevertheless allow thieves to come into their homes and steal their children's hearts. The body of the child is left there, but the heart is being stolen by television, cell phones, tablets, and other media gadgets. A steady stream of music containing violent or sensual lyrics, various forms of pornography, and violent video games are ingested by the child's psyche—and we wonder why they don't follow the Lord in later years.

Jesus prayed that we might be *in* the world but not *of* the world, just as He was. He knew—as we should—that there is a world out there that is hostile toward God. Elsewhere, John defines it as "the desires of the flesh and the desires of the eyes and pride of life" (1 John 2:16). This world, John adds, "is passing away along with its desires, but whoever does the will of God abides forever" (v. 17).

We can't break the addictive power of modern technology with its stream of worldly entertainment without consistent, focused spiritual warfare. The lust or desire of the flesh, the lure of covetousness, and the pride of possessions and appearance—these fight against God. John said it clearly, "If anyone loves the world, the love of the Father is not in him" (v. 15).

We must pray for ourselves and our children that we would be kept from evil: "but as he who called you is holy, you also be holy in all your conduct" (1 Peter 1:15).

Let Us Pray

Father, I throw myself at Your feet, imploring You to deliver me and my child from both the overt and subtle intrusions of the world into our lives. Help me to break with any sinful avenues that I frequently choose, so that I might not seek to satisfy my desires apart from Your holiness.

I pray for my child who is bound in their addiction to television, pornography, and/or violence. Show them that these sins always leave a bitter aftertaste, and that although they promise like a god, they pay like the devil. I pray that my child might be willing to close all the open doors by which the world is invited into their hearts.

But Father, they are bound, slaves to sin, and slaves cannot set themselves free. Your word tells us, "Truly, truly, I say to you, everyone who practices sin is a slave to sin . . . . if the Son sets you free, you will be free indeed" (John 8:34, 36). I claim this promise.

So, come in power to rescue and deliver them. In faith, I withstand the power of Satan, the "god of this world."

Even as You prayed, so I pray, "Keep them from the evil one."

Give all of us a passion for Jesus that is greater than our passion to sin.

In Jesus' name, Amen.

WEDNESDAY: A PRAYER FOR FREEDOM FROM SELF-INCRIMINATION

"Who shall bring any charge against God's elect? It is God who justifies. Who is to condemn? Christ Jesus is the one who died—more than that, who was raised— who is at the right hand of God, who indeed is interceding for us" (Rom. 8:33–34).

There are millions of people who go to church on Sunday and confess their sins, but they are not converted as a result of this exercise. If we had to confess all of our sins in order to be saved, salvation would be beyond reach. For one thing, we may be committing sins that we don't even realize are sins. For another, we can't remember all of our sins, and even if we could, tomorrow is another day bringing new sins. It would be like wiping the floor while the faucet is overflowing!

Let us pray that our children will understand the beauty and power of the gospel.

When God saves us, He has to absolve us from all of our sins—past, present, and future—in one divine act. He does this by crediting us with the righteousness of Jesus Christ in response to saving faith. By that act, we are legally perfect forever.

Twenty-four hours a day, God demands that we be perfect if He is to fellowship with us and welcome us into heaven at death; twenty-four hours a day Jesus Christ supplies what

God demands. Jesus stands in for us and we are accepted as if we were Him.

Yes, of course, as Christians we confess our sins to maintain fellowship with God, but our legal standing remains unchanged despite our continuing struggles with sin and failure. The unchangeable righteousness of Christ, once it's credited to us, is never diminished nor removed from us.

So who can bring a charge against God's elect? Your conscience can. Other people can. And of course, there's the devil, who accuses the saints day and night. In response, Paul says, "It is God who justifies." What is more, Jesus, even now, intercedes for us. Only such assurance silences our conscience—our judge within.

Personally, I rely on this truth every day: my heavenly Father sees me as being "in Christ," and thereby my guilt is removed and my conscience is stilled. We must pray that we and other believers will depend on this blessed reality whenever we are overcome by regret and guilt.

Let Us Pray

Father, open my eyes to the reality that Christ's righteousness is mine. May I, despite my struggles with sin, rejoice that Jesus represents me to You. Though I mourn over my sins, may I not be disheartened. Help me look to Jesus and not my own performance as the basis of my acceptance.

I pray for my child that they might be satisfied with what Jesus has done; may they be freed from the condemnation of sin, and rest in the assurance that they've been accepted in the Beloved One. Each morning, let them rise to renew their confidence in the promise that Jesus has made them pleasing and acceptable to You. May the discouragement that so often leads to a spiral of sin vanish when they remember that no one can bring a charge against God's elect without being met by the declaration that they have been justified.

So I pray for them as I pray for myself, that we might believe the promise that "It is God who justifies" and Jesus takes away our condemnation by His death, resurrection, and ascension (see Rom. 8:33–34).

May I use these verses when I feel discouraged or cannot forgive myself. And may my freedom be an inspiration to my children.

In Jesus' name, Amen.

THURSDAY: A PRAYER FOR PURITY

"Or do you not know that your body is a temple of the Holy Spirit within you, whom you have from God? You are not your own, for you were bought with a price. So glorify God in your body" (1 Cor. 6:19–20).

Sin—particularly known sin—defiles the conscience, which in turn leads to more sin.

In context, Paul is chastising the church at Corinth because they had allowed an immoral relationship to continue without disciplining the offenders. Paul chides them for not mourning over their failure, instead continuing with business as usual and even bragging about how great their church was. But God will not stand by without some form of discipline and judgment of His own. In such a case, the whole church suffers. Public sin must have some kind of public discipline.

We must remind our children that sexual sins have particularly far-reaching personal consequences. The sexual relationship binds two people together in a "soul-tie" that cannot be wished away. True, all sin is sin and needs forgiveness and cleansing. But some sins have worse consequences for the soul. If your child has fallen into the sin of immorality, let them know that God's arms are wide open to welcome them back into fellowship.

Without deep repentance and accountability, this behavior will almost surely be committed again and again. Only God can do what needs to be done.

Let Us Pray

Father, we admit that we are a sinful people; we admit that we often sin in thought, word, and deed. We pray that You might cleanse us, no matter how painful. We pray that we will be honest about our sins and remember this admonition: "Therefore go out from their midst, and be separate from them, says the Lord, and touch no unclean thing; then I will welcome you, and I will be a father to you, and you shall be sons and daughters to me, says the Lord Almighty" (2 Cor. 6:17–18).

Father, Your word reminds us that we are most easily deceived by our passions. After listing various sexual sins, we are warned, "Let no one deceive you with empty words, for because of these things the wrath of God comes upon the sons of disobedience" (Eph. 5:6). Show all of us the deceptions of immorality and sexual indiscretions. Reveal to us what we don't see because of our propensity to self-justification.

I pray for my children. O God, keep them from evil, especially the lure of sexual sin. Again I pray, Lord, give them a passion for You that is greater than their passion to sin. Rid them of the hypocrisy of living in two worlds; make them genuine and submissive, remembering that it is the pure in heart who see God.

Every day may we be reminded that our bodies are a temple in which You dwell. And these bodies are not ours to misuse or contaminate. I pray we shall always seek to glorify You in our bodies.

In Jesus' name, Amen.

FRIDAY: A PRAYER TO GRASP

THEIR IDENTIFICATION WITH JESUS CHRIST

"I have been crucified with Christ. It is no longer I who live, but Christ who lives in me. And the life I now live in the flesh I live by faith in the Son of God, who loved me and gave himself for me" (Gal. 2:20).

Our children need to understand that the changes God makes in our lives after our conversion are profound and lasting; God does a deep work that rituals cannot perform. Consider this: God so profoundly put us into Jesus—in a legal way—that His history becomes our history. We were crucified with Him, and "we shall certainly be united with him in a resurrection like his" (Rom. 6:5). This identification with Christ is the basis for our intimate relationship with Him; it is also the basis of our walk of victory.

If you were convicted of a capital crime and then put to death for it, the law would have no more claim on you. Just so, as believers, we've died with Christ, and as a result, we are dead to our obligations to meet the demands of the law. In short, Jesus fulfilled the demands of the law for us. Our "death" with Jesus frees us from a standard we could never keep and the punishments that accompany it. Thanks be, we still live but we do so by faith in Jesus.

"The true Christian life," writes John MacArthur, "is not so much a believer's living for Christ as Christ's living through a believer."[13] Before our conversion, we did the best we could at managing our guilt and hoping that we could rectify our relationship with God. After our conversion, we continue to strive, but with an entirely different motivation: now we're empowered by letting Christ live in and through us. Our responsibility is to surrender with confidence so that the life we now live, we live by "faith in the Son of God" who loved us and gave Himself for us.

This "crucified life," as it's sometimes called, means that we not only died to the Law in Christ, but we must by faith die to our own plans and ambitions; now our lives are entirely in His capable hands. Letting Christ live in us opens up a whole spectrum of hope and victory.

The bottom line: we are saved by faith in Christ who *died* for us; now we continue to have faith in the Christ who *lives* for us and in us. Let us not concentrate as much on living for Christ as trusting Christ to live in us! And let us pray we will understand and obey.

We must pray that we and our children will understand this and seek to depend on Christ at all times. It is much easier when we realize that God has already done everything necessary for us to simply accept our union with Christ.

Let Us Pray

Father, I begin by asking that I will grasp the meaning of this verse, that the demands of the law have been met on my behalf by Jesus Christ. But equally wonderful, let me also have confidence that Jesus now lives in me. Let me exercise the same faith in the living Christ within me as I have for the Christ who died for me. Let the thought that Christ lives within me captivate my mind and heart and that I might walk in the light of this experience.

Also, Father, I pray for my child who is presently living for himself/herself. I pray that they might submit to Jesus who lives within them. And if they do not know Him as Savior, I pray that they will receive His gift of grace and accept Him as their Savior and Lord. Father, do a work in their heart that is miraculous and lasting.

Overcome hidden crevasses of deceit and darkness. We need your Holy Spirit to show us what we can't see on our own. Today we rejoice that we have been (past tense) crucified with Christ and that Christ lives in us.

Father, help us believe that Christ living within us frees us from the senseless pressures of life. Help us let You take charge and work through us for Your glory.

In Jesus' name, Amen.

SATURDAY: A PRAYER
FOR SPIRITUAL ENLIGHTENMENT

"I do not cease to give thanks for you, remembering
you in my prayers, that the God of our Lord Jesus
Christ, the Father of glory, may give you the Spirit of
wisdom and of revelation in the knowledge of him,
having the eyes of your hearts enlightened, that you
may know what is the hope to which he has called you,
what are the riches of his glorious inheritance in the
saints, and what is the immeasurable greatness of his
power toward us who believe . . ." (Eph. 1:16–19).

Our children need to learn to pray scriptural prayers. We
need to teach them that prayer is more than bringing a list
of requests to God. Certainly, there are times when we must
add the words, "if it be Your will" at the end of our prayers.
When Jesus was in Gethsemane He prayed, "Not my will,
but Your will be done." However, there are prayers we can
pray where we do not have to add "if it be Your will" because
we know that we are praying right in line with God's will; in
other words, we are praying God's will exactly.

Today, we will pray God's revealed will for our children.
No need to add, "if it is Your will." Paul did not pray that
the believers in Ephesus be rich, or that they be physically
healed, or even that they might be kept from suffering and
persecution. But when we pray for the spiritual realities for
which Paul prayed, then we know that we are praying God's

will back to Him. This is God's will for all of His people in all ages.

The prayer we will be praying for our children is among the grandest that we could ever pray for ourselves and others. If we prayed this prayer each day, we could never exhaust its depths, and we would soon see that we need these realities each day, twenty-four hours a day, seven days a week, 365 days a year.

The story has been told that William Randolph Hearst once read about an extremely valuable piece of art that he thought should be added to his extensive collection. He instructed his agent to find it and acquire it at any price. Eventually, the agent reported that the piece was already in Hearst's own warehouse and had actually been his for many years!

Just so, most of the blessings we pray for are already our inheritance as God's children, and along with Paul, we should pray that the believers might understand what they have already been given in Christ—the power and the experiences they have been longing for already belong to them.

Let us pray this prayer for ourselves and our children. You will discover unexpected strength and blessing from praying it back to God. As God answers, our children will be blessed. In the end, we do not have to say, "If it be Your will!"

Let Us Pray

Father, I thank You for Paul, who not only had a burden to pray for Your people, but also, by divine revelation, understood what Your will is for each of us. So I pray You might now give me freedom in praying this prayer for my child that they might come to experience all the blessings that belong to us by faith in Christ.

Lord, expand my child's vision and understanding, as I pray for them from this rich treasure of Your Word (see Eph. 1:16–23). Father, reveal to all of us what we cannot grasp by human wisdom; show us the boundless treasures we have in our triumphant Lord Jesus Christ.

In Jesus' name, Amen.

SUNDAY: A PRAYER FOR SUNDAY
. . . AND FOR SUNDAYS TO COME!

"And it is my prayer that your love may abound more
and more, with knowledge and all discernment, so that
you may approve what is excellent, and so be pure and
blameless for the day of Christ, filled with the fruit of
righteousness that comes through Jesus Christ,
to the glory and praise of God" (Phil. 1:9–11).

There are some prayers that are so encompassing, so
God-honoring, and so continually appropriate that they
can be prayed regularly, whether daily or weekly. Each time
they can be prayed with renewed meaning and grace. Such
prayers always express God's will.

On his second missionary journey, Paul established the
church in Philippi. As we read his letter to this church, we
are given a window into his heart and into the heart of God.
Reread this prayer carefully, taking note of its requests.

First, he prays "that their love may abound"—that love
might overflow in their hearts like a river overflows its banks.
This presupposes that people would deal with their bitterness,
anger, etc. Love would replace their selfishness, jealousy, and
impatience with others. This love is not just sentimentality;
it is a willingness to choose that which is right for us and for
others, and to do so joyfully.

This love is accompanied with knowledge. Paul always
prayed that the people would have an informed love that

could, at times, require toughness. Such love knows to forgive. It knows the best way to navigate difficult relationships; it is infused with wisdom and knowledge.

It's also a love accompanied by discernment. It's not just being able to distinguish right from wrong, but to be able to identify that which is best; it is a love that approves of that which is excellent. Discerning love means that we know when our love requires toughness; it is not a love that fails to expect accountability.

Love without discernment leads to rewriting Scripture to suit our own wishes. Thus, under the banner of love, some affirm same-sex relationships or approve of social programs that actually hinder rather than help the poor. In the Bible, love is not left without guidelines. As Jesus said, "If you love me, you will keep my commandments."

Because divine love is contrary to our selfish nature, it is truly an act of God. Only God can cause us to love the unlovable; only divine love can love without expecting to be loved in return. You want to pray for your child? Pray that they will have knowledgeable, discerning love.

Second, Paul prays that this divine love will result in purity, "to be pure and blameless for the day of Christ." In other words, love should have this ultimate result. The Greek word for purity comes from the word "sun." It is a purity tested by the light of the sun.

Paul is praying that we might be able to stand in the sunlight. This affects how we use our free time and how we invest our lives in all that is around us. We are tested by God's sunlight in a very dark world. And we must ask, when the sunlight of God shines in our hearts, what is revealed?

Paul connects this purity with being "blameless for the day of Christ"—that we might stand before Christ without offense. That means we diligently deal with our sins as they arise in our hearts. "And now, little children, abide in him, so that when he appears we may have confidence and not shrink from him in shame at his coming" (1 John 2:28).

Finally, Paul prays that they will have greater fruit. "Filled with the fruit of righteousness that comes through Jesus Christ, to the glory and praise of God" (Phil. 1:11). In other words, our conduct should be such that God receives the glory in what we think, say, and do. Fruit is the expression of the inner nature; it is the product of the grace of God. As we grow in grace, we grow in fruit.

The bottom line is that we must pray that we will live for a better world. In summary, we must pray for love, purity, and fruit. Corporate prayer reinforces what we already pray in private. When we call on God for ourselves and others, He will hear.

Let Us Pray

Let us read Paul's prayer on behalf of ourselves and our children:

"And it is my prayer that your love may abound more and more, with knowledge and all discernment, so that you may approve what is excellent, and so be pure and blameless for the day of Christ, filled with the fruit of righteousness that comes through Jesus Christ, to the glory and praise of God" (Phil. 1:9–11).

In Jesus' name, Amen.

A Prayer
Beyond Your Family
for the Nation

Praying for our children means that we should also pray for the world that they are growing up in. Today, we are raising our children in Babylon; we are a minority in the midst of a majority pagan culture. When the Israelites were exiled to Babylon, they were commanded to seek the welfare of this pagan city and to "pray to the LORD" for its people (Jer. 29:7). They were to pray for their cruel captors whose armies captured Jerusalem, killed many Jews, and for sport threw Jewish babies against the rocks. We must teach our children to pray for our enemies, just as we must teach them to pray for their classmates, for their peers, and for their country.

We as parents could all wish that our children would grow up to be as faithful in prayer as Daniel was when he was among the captives forced to live in Babylon. He had a consistent prayer life beginning with his arrival as a teenager of about seventeen years of age. Early on he was even an advisor to the evil King Nebuchadnezzar whose cruel armies had captured Jerusalem. As an older man in his eighties, Daniel became a trusted advisor to another king named Darius who was planning to promote his loyal servant.

Some of the governors of the kingdom became jealous of Daniel and plotted his demise. They knew that Darius had reserved a den of hungry lions for anyone who refused to obey his orders. These evil men were so incensed by Daniel's prayer life that they persuaded the King to make a decree that "whoever makes petition to any god or man for thirty days, except to you, O king, shall be cast into the den of lions" (Dan. 6:7).

Darius signed the order.

But Daniel feared God more than the lion's den!

"When Daniel knew that the document had been signed, he went to his house where he had windows in his upper chamber open toward Jerusalem. He got down on his knees three times a day and prayed and gave thanks before his God, as he had done previously" (6:10). We all know that God sent an angel to close the mouths of the lions. But—and this is critical—Daniel had no such assurances when he was thrown into that dungeon. Whether in his life or through his death, Daniel desired to bring glory to God.

Paganism despises religious tolerance. Daniel was not intruding on anyone else's right to worship whatever god they chose. He was not compelling pagans to believe in Jehovah; he was not even praying in a public place where he might be a nuisance to those who passed by. He was in his own house, kneeling alone to pray and worship. But that was not good enough for those who hated Daniel, the faithful servant of the God of Abraham, Isaac, and Jacob.

I wish we'd been there to hear Daniel pray. With the threat of the lion's den in his future, he no doubt prayed desperate prayers. Nothing focuses the mind, according to Samuel Johnson, like the knowledge that one is to be "hanged in a fortnight."[14] I doubt that Daniel prayed only for deliverance; most likely he prayed for faithfulness. His life was not in the hands of the king (or the paws of the lions!) but in God's care.

The lesson for us is clear: Let us not be intimidated by a culture that wants to prohibit our obedience to God and our worship of Him. Let us not back off when laws are made that compel us to compromise our conscience or silence our witness. We will not be thrown into a lion's den, but we might be ostracized, lose our jobs, or be fined. Or shamed.

Daniel's extended prayer in 9:3–19 reveals what he prayed while in Babylon. His prayer was dominated by two themes: the righteousness of God and the sin of the nation of Israel.

He pleads for undeserved mercy: "We have sinned and done wrong and acted wickedly and rebelled, turning aside from your commandments and rules. We have not listened to your servants the prophets, who spoke in your name . . . To you, O Lord, belongs righteousness but to us open shame" (vv. 5, 6, 7a).

Interestingly, he did not pray for the Babylonians, though undoubtedly he prayed for them on other occasions. His primary concern was for the people who were "called by God's name." The New Testament follows the same pattern. Read Paul's prayers. They were for believers that they might walk in obedience and faith. The culture can't be changed until people are changed. *The world can't be made right until believers are made right.*

Daniel learned that earnest prayer also attracts the opposition of the spirit world. For three weeks he mourned, fasted, and prayed with no visible results. Then in a terrifying vision, he heard a voice that assured him that his prayer had been heard as soon as it had been uttered, but the answer was delayed because "the prince of the kingdom of Persia" withstood the messenger until the angel Gabriel came to his rescue (10:13). Evidently an evil spirit, perhaps Satan himself who was trying to direct the policies of the kingdom of Persia, tried to block the revelation that Daniel was about to receive. But Daniel persisted and the answer came.

When we read Daniel's prayer, we can't help being convicted

of the need to pray beyond our own lives and families. This is not a time for us to pray prayers of blessing without prayers of deep repentance. We have to call on God on behalf of His church, and yes, our nation, and God's witness in the world. Corrie Ten Boom said, "The wonderful thing about praying is that you leave a world of not being able to do something, and enter God's realm where everything is possible."[15]

And if we have no burden to pray? We wait before God until He shares His will with us.

In preparation for this section, I decided to read Daniel's prayer each day for a week substituting the church and America for the references to the nation Israel. My own heart was challenged, and the burden I have for our country increased. I discovered that Daniel said it better than I could: "'For we do not present our pleas before you because of our righteousness, but because of your great mercy'" (Dan. 9:18).

If we as Christians were to spend as much time praying for the enemies of Christianity as we do complaining about them, we might yet be amazed at what God would do in our country. As a result of Daniel's prayer, God answered and brought the Israelites from Babylon back into the land. God often does work without our prayers, but our intercession moves His hand.

Prayer is not just saying the right words; it is having the right heart. We must begin confessing our own prayerlessness before we begin to earnestly pray. The distractions of

Babylon must be set aside to focus on what is most important. Our survival is at stake.

The time to repent is now.

Let us Pray

This prayer takes excerpts from Daniel's prayer and makes it applicable for our nation.

"O Lord, the great and awesome God, who keeps covenant and steadfast love with those who love Him and keep His commandments, we have sinned and done wrong and acted wickedly and rebelled, turning aside from Your commandments and rules. We have not listened to Your servants the prophets who spoke in Your name to our kings, our princes, and our fathers, and to all the people of the land. To You, O Lord, belongs righteousness, but to us open shame . . . we have rebelled . . .

And now, O Lord our God, listen to the prayer of Your servant and to his plea for mercy, and for Your own sake, O Lord, make Your face shine upon [our nation conceived in liberty but now in rebellion to Your laws and statues] . . . . for we do not present our pleas before You because of our righteousness, but because of Your great mercy . . ."

O God, we as a nation have normalized perversion; we have glorified what You have condemned. We as

Your people have been intimidated; we have become silent at a time when we should be speaking. Help us, O God, to be the church that we should be!"

Let me suggest that you now pray a similar prayer for your city, your school district, and for our local and national leadership.

In Jesus' name, Amen.

Should I Fast for My Child?

Persistent prayer has a purpose. It is a test that we might draw closer to God. We must insist that Satan will flee, and we must pray in faith. Your child may have rejected you or left your home, but that child has not left your heart. Thanks to God's omnipotence, you have an advantage in the life of your child, for you can pray.

Should you fast for yourself and your children? Fasting is mentioned at least fifty times in the Bible. Moses fasted, Daniel fasted, the prophets fasted, Nehemiah fasted, Jesus fasted, Paul fasted—all the apostles and the early church fasted. Still we may think these examples don't apply to us. We may think that fasting went the way of medieval mysticism and the monastery, that the practice has all but disappeared in the church.

Yet Jesus did not say, "*If* you fast, do not look gloomy like the hypocrites, for they disfigure their faces that their fasting may be seen by others . . ." (Matt. 6:16). Rather, Jesus said, "And *when* you fast . . ." In other words, He assumed His disciples would fast. He certainly cannot make that assumption about today's church members. Announce a *feast* and you can expect that many will respond; announce a *fast* and few will accept the invitation.

Of course, there are misconceptions about fasting that we must avoid. Fasting does not manipulate a reluctant God to act. David fasted when he was told that his child was going to die. In fact, the Bible says that he went out and lay on the ground beseeching God, and yet the child died. Fasting does not manipulate God to do our bidding.

Fasting does not give us special merit before God. Fasting does not "balance the scales" and make us look a little better before God in light of the sacrifice we have made. We've already learned that Jesus denounced those who wanted to make themselves look spiritual by fasting. He said that rather than fasting to be seen by others, "anoint your head and wash your face, that your fasting may *not* be seen by others but by your Father who is in secret. And your Father who sees in secret will reward you" (Matt. 6:17–18). Don't believe this syllogism: "Pious people fast; I am fasting; therefore, I must be pious."

In Old Testament times, God sometimes told those who were fasting to stop it! "Behold, in the day of your fast you seek your own pleasure, and oppress all your workers. Behold, you fast only to quarrel and to fight and to hit with a wicked fist. Fasting like yours this day will not make your voice to be heard on high" (Isa. 58:3–4). Their fasting did not move God to answer any of their prayers. In fact, their sacrifice only increased His displeasure with their religious practices. The reason? Their fasting was just a ritual; it was an attempt to convince God to give them what they wanted.

God responded, saying in effect, "If your fasting doesn't change your heart, and does not increase the amount of love that you have in your heart and your ability to do good works, then stop the charade! I can't stand this outward act of fasting unless it brings about an inner change."

Fasting is a full-body response to God, usually at a critical time and a time of desperation. But fasting may also be done with regularity, such as one day a week. The Bible says nothing about the physical benefits of fasting (though there are many), but only emphasizes the spiritual benefits.

The prophet Joel encourages fasting if it is done properly and for the right reasons. "Consecrate a fast; call a solemn assembly. Gather the elders and all the inhabitants of the land to the house of the Lord your God, and cry out to the Lord" (Joel 1:14). Things were desperate and called for desperate prayer and crying out to God. But there was to be a specific reason for this fasting: it was to bring about repentance.

God continues, "'Yet even now,' declares the LORD, 'return to me with all your heart, with fasting, with weeping, and with mourning; and rend your hearts and not your garments'" (2:12–13). That last phrase can be understood if we remember that the people would often tear their clothes as an expression of their desperation, but it was more for show and did not bring about a change of heart. God was saying, "Don't tear your clothes; tear your hearts." God was continually pointing the people from the outward to the inward; from the body to the heart. Understand that the real purpose of fasting is a deeper kind of repentance.

Our fasting should reveal our sin. Hunger pangs should bring us to a deep mourning, not just for food, but for the cleansing of God. Fasting also enables us to have heightened spiritual sensitivity and become aware that we are in a spiritual battle. After Jesus fasted for forty days and forty nights in the desert, the devil came to Him. Don't be surprised that the devil shows up when you fast.

Fasting is a discipline I practice occasionally just to give God an extended opportunity to search my heart. Even when it is for simply a day or two, my hunger makes me remember that I need God more than I need food. God wants me to focus on my heart, not my body.

When we fast, we must seek God's face, not just His hand. We all would like to have God answer our prayer. "Lord, I have a son who isn't following you. I've got financial issues. I have a health matter that frightens me . . ." These requests are legitimate, but the primary purpose of fasting is to seek God and not seek quick answers. We can easily be like a child who makes requests but never looks into the parent's face—a child who reaches out to take the money from the father's hand without so much as glancing into the father's eyes. During fasting, it is our relationship with our heavenly Father that should be the focus of our attention.

Seeking God in humble submission is our greatest privilege. Only then do our prayer requests fall into place. Jesus said, "But seek first the kingdom of God and his righteousness, and all these things will be added to you" (Matt. 6:33).

Joel chided the people for fasting without repentance, but Jeremiah gave them this word of encouragement from God: "You will seek me and find me, when you seek me with all your heart" (Jer. 29:13).

Fast for your children, but fast primarily for yourself. Or, more accurately, fast for God; fast for His glory and your more intimate relationship with Him.

"Beware in your prayer, above everything else, of limiting God, not only by unbelief, but by fancying that you know what He can do."[16]

God responds to the desperate and blesses the repentant. *Keep praying!*

Acknowledgments

As I have learned through years of writing, a book is always a community project! Micah Shumate, thanks for insisting that I write this, and Letricia Brooks, thanks for editing what became the first edition published by the Moody Church Media Ministry.

Duane Sherman, you encouraged me to have the book published by Moody Publishers so that it would have a wider audience. Amanda Cleary Eastep, your help in editing, footnoting, and, when necessary, rewriting was indispensable in getting this book ready for publication. You also encouraged me by saying, "This book is a mighty sword in the hands of praying parents."

Most importantly, I am grateful to Jesus Christ who gives us access to the throne room of God. I only pray that we as parents will take advantage of this marvelous opportunity and that our children will bear witness that our prayers for them have been answered.

Notes

1. Neil Anderson, "Praying for Your Children," Freedom in Christ, https://ficm.org/wp-content/uploads/2013/04/PrayingForYourChildren.pdf.

2. Gary Smalley and John Trent, *The Gift of Blessing* (Nashville: Thomas Nelson Publishers, 1986), 24.

3. Jim Cymbala, *Breakthrough Prayer* (Grand Rapids: Zondervan, 2003), 84.

4. Augustine, *The Confessions of St. Augustine* (Chicago: Moody Publishers, 2007), 77.

5. Ibid., 74.

6. Ibid., 77.

7. William Barclay, *Gospel of Matthew*, vol. 2 (Westminster, KY: John Knox Press, 2002), 142.

8. Iris Delgado, *Satan, You Can't Have My Children* (Lake Mary, FL: Charisma Media, 2011), 6. I might not agree with all that Iris Delgado has written, but her determination and story of answered prayer is an encouragement to me.

9. Ibid., 19.

10. E. M. Bounds, *E. M. Bounds, The Classic Collection on Prayer* (Newberry, FL: Bridge-Logos Publishers, 2001), 443, 518.

11. Lee Weeks, "From the Pit to the Pulpit," *Decision Magazine*, June 1, 2019, https://decisionmagazine.com/from-pit-to-pulpit/.

12. Ibid.

13. John MacArthur, *Galatians*, MacArthur New Testament Commentary (Chicago: Moody Publishers, 1987), 60.

14. James Boswell, *The Life of Samuel Johnson*, vol. 3, 194, https://books .google.com/books?id=f8GJA-nBcE0C&printsec=frontcover&dq= boswell%27s+life+of+johnson&hl=en&newbks=1&newbks_redir= 0&sa=X&ved=2ahUKEwiWuN_7gd7mAhXUUs0KHRD5AfIQ6 AEwB3oECAgQAg#v=onepage&q=hanged%20in%20a%20fortnight &f=false.

15. Corrie Ten Boom, *I Stand at the Door and Knock* (Grand Rapids: Zondervan, 2008), 95.

16. Andrew Murray, *The Ministry of Intercession: A Plea for More Prayer* (Chicago: Revell, 1898), 220.

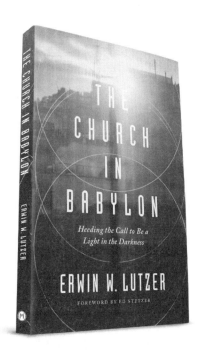

HOW TO RAISE A GODLY MAN,
NOT A FULL-GROWN BOY.

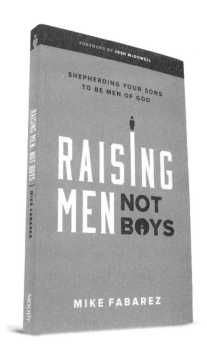

Raising Men, Not Boys is about navigating the times and raising a generation of men on godly principles—sons who are ready, able, and motivated to represent God during their days of sojourn on this earth. Parents will be equipped to set the spiritual trajectory of sons so that they launch into godly manhood, rather than flounder in prolonged immaturity.

978-0-8024-1657-5 | also available as eBook and audiobook

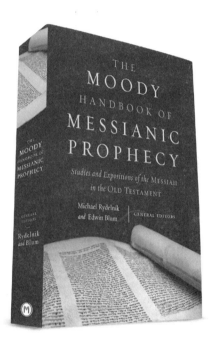